CRAFT ATTACK!

TEXTILE CRAFTS

Annalees Lim

Gareth Stevens
Publishing

Please visit our website, www.garethstevens.com. For a free color catalog of all our high-quality books, call toll free 1-800-542-2595 or fax 1-877-542-2596.

Library of Congress Cataloging-in-Publication Data

Lim, Annalees.
Textile crafts / by Annalees Lim.
    pages cm. — (Craft attack)
Includes bibliographical references and index.
ISBN 978-1-4824-3301-2 (pbk.)
ISBN 978-1-4824-0222-3 (6-pack)
ISBN 978-1-4824-0224-7 (library binding)
1. Textile crafts—Juvenile literature. I. Title.
TT712.L56 2014
745.5—dc23

                                    2013021484

First Edition

Published in 2014 by
Gareth Stevens Publishing
111 East 14th Street, Suite 349
New York, NY 10003

Copyright © 2014 Arcturus Publishing

Editors: Joe Harris and Sara Gerlings
Design: Elaine Wilkinson
Cover design: Elaine Wilkinson
Photography: Simon Pask

Printed in the United States of America

CPSIA compliance information: Batch #CW14GS: For further information contact Gareth Stevens, New York, New York at 1-800-542-2595.

CONTENTS

TERRIFIC TEXTILES

Making textile crafts is much easier than most people think… and it's also lots of fun! Please make sure that you ask an adult to help you with your first few projects, and always remember to be careful with pins and needles.

SIMPLE STITCHES

Before you start you might need to learn a few basic stitches!

Tacking Stitch
This stitch is used to temporarily hold two pieces of fabric together. It is then removed when you have finished your neat stitches. Make sure you have put a knot in the thread and make long, loose stitches that go in and out of the fabric.

Running Stitch
This is a neater version of the tacking stitch, which looks better in a finished project and can be used for decoration.

First tie a knot in your thread (you should do this for all permanent stitches), then sew two small stitches on top of each other. Push the needle in and out of the fabric, making sure that each stitch and the gap between the stitches are the same length. To finish, tie a knot in the thread at the back of the fabric before you cut off the unused part of the thread with scissors.

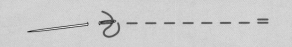

Back Stitch

A back stitch is similar to a running stitch but without the gaps. Make your first stitch in the same way as you would with a running stitch. Then push the needle up through the fabric, but instead of moving it forwards to make the next stitch, push it back through the hole you made with the previous stitch and back up again in front of the stitch. Repeat this all along the fabric.

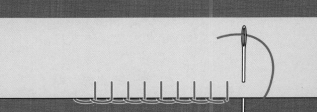

Blanket Stitch and Whip Stitch

These are used to attach two pieces of fabric together. A whip stitch is very simple—you just loop the thread around and around in a spiral, passing it through the fabric. A blanket stitch (shown left) is a little more advanced. Pass the needle up through the fabric, making sure that it is at least 0.4 inch (1 cm) from the edge. Then pass the needle through the back of the fabric again 0.4 inch (1 cm) along and start to pull the needle and thread through the fabric. Stop when you have made a small loop and pass the needle through the loop you have just made.

YOUR TOOLKIT

Needle and Thread

These are essential items. You will need a sharp needle with a large enough eye for you to pass thread through. Ask an adult to help you the first time you use a needle, so that you don't prick yourself.

Scissors

A small pair of normal craft scissors will work fine for the projects in this book. They just need to be sturdy enough to cut through fabric.

Felt and Fabric

The important difference between felt and fabric is that fabric frays and felt does not. Most of the time, you will want to avoid leaving a raw (unstitched) fabric edge, because if you do this your project will not last as long. Felt is easy to cut and you can either stick it together with fabric glue or sew it together with a needle and thread.

CUTE SOCK OWLS

Where do all those missing socks disappear to? You can make use of odd socks by turning them into lovable owls.

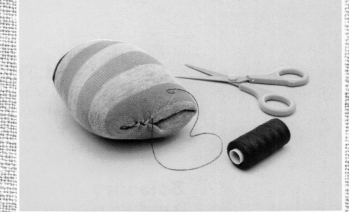

1 Choose a colorful sock and pack it with cushion stuffing until it is half full.

2 Tuck in the open end of the sock, and sew a few whip stitches to hold it in place. Tie a knot and snip off the loose end of the thread.

3 Using scissors, cut these shapes from felt: a large triangle for the face, two small triangles for the beak, two wings, two circles for eyes, two feet, and two feather shapes.

4 Sew all the felt shapes—except the beak—to your sock with your needle and thread, using a whip stitch.

5 Sew on the two small triangles to form the beak. Only sew on the short end of each triangle, so that the beak stands out from the face.

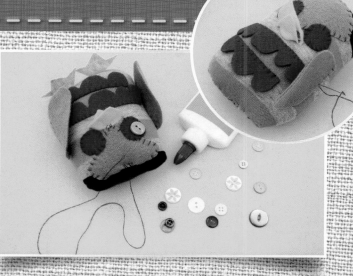

6 Use fabric glue for the eyes. Glue a small button (the pupil) on top of a medium-sized button (the eye). Pinch the top of the owl together and sew together to make the ears.

ROCK STAR RAG DOLL

This punk rock rag doll may be made from scrap material, but he's got some real rock star attitude! You could try making a doll that looks like a cute mini version of a real performer.

You will need:

felt
brightly colored fabric
(use old bit of clothes
or scraps from other
projects)
cushion stuffing
colored yarn
needle and thread
scissors

1 Cut out two circles, two squares, four long rectangles, and four short rectangles from your scrap fabric.

2 Now cut shapes out of felt to make details such as eyes and patterns on the clothing. Sew them on with a running stitch. You may want to use a brightly colored thread.

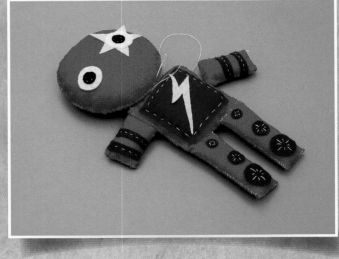

3 Use a whip stitch to sew matching pairs of shapes together to make the head, body, arms, and legs. Make sure that the right sides of the fabric are facing outwards. Leave a 2-inch (5 cm) gap along one edge of each of your pairs. Stuff each of your body parts with cushion stuffing, then sew up the gap.

4 Use a whip stitch again to sew all the pieces together to make the body.

5 Cut a handful of yarn to the same length and tie the pieces together in the middle. Sew them onto the head of your doll.

TOADSTOOL DOORSTOP

This bean bag creation will prop your door open... and add a little fun to your room. A toadstool doorstop, complete with fluttering butterfly, also makes a great gift!

You will need:

red, white, and green cotton fabric
needle and thread
sturdy corduroy
large buttons
dried beans
sturdy scissors
tape measure
pins
felt

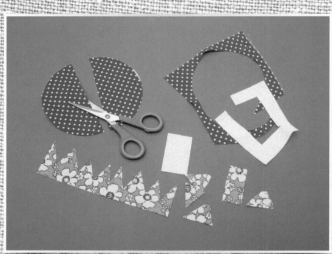

1 Cut two squares of corduroy fabric measuring 8 x 8 inches (20 x 20 cm), and four rectangles measuring 4 x 8 inches (10 x 20 cm). Use a sturdy pair of scissors for this.

2 Cut out a semicircle of red cotton fabric, a rectangle of white cotton, and a zigzag shape from the green fabric for the grass. You don't need to measure the pieces, but they must fit on a corduroy square.

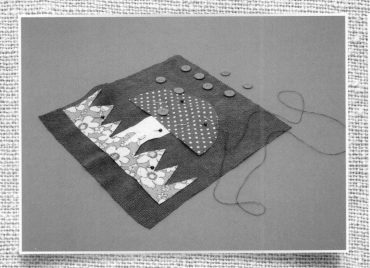

3 Use pins to fix the shapes in place on one of the corduroy squares. Then sew them on using a running or whip stitch. Sew on some large buttons for the toadstool's spots.

4 Sew the corduroy pieces together to make a box shape. It must be stitched together inside out, with the square sides facing each other. Remember to leave a 2-inch (5 cm) gap in the stitching along one side.

5 Turn the doorstop right-side out and fill it with dried beans. Sew up the gap in the stitching to keep all the filling in place. Cut a butterfly shape from felt, and sew it onto the corner of the doorstop.

FUNKY FELT FRIEND

This colorful little chap is always ready to cheer you up with his happy smile. You could hang him in your window or use a looped thread to make him into a phone charm.

You will need:

felt in several colors
cushion stuffing
large roll of tape
needle and thread
tape measure
pen and paper
scissors and pins

1 Trace the roll of tape onto a piece of paper. Design your felt friend inside the circle.

2 Cut out the circle with scissors. Trace around it twice onto felt. Cut out your felt circles carefully.

3 Cut along the lines of your paper design to make smaller shapes. Trace around them onto felt of different colors. Cut all the felt shapes out. Then sew your smaller felt pieces onto one of the felt circles, using a running stitch.

4 Sew the two circles together using a blanket stitch, with the right sides facing out, leaving a 1-inch (3 cm) gap along the side. Keep the needle and thread attached, but pin the needle to the felt to keep it safe.

5 Fill the circle with stuffing, then finish sewing up the side.

COCOA COZY

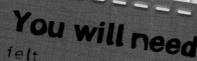

Keep your mug of cocoa warm with a handmade cozy. It turns a plain mug into something crafty, colorful, and fun! It's easy to take off when you need to wash it.

You will need

felt
buttons
elastic
needle and thread
scissors
cloth tape measure
mug

1 Measure around your mug with a cloth tape measure. Measure its height too. Cut a piece of felt that will wrap around the mug, but make it 0.8 inch (2 cm) shorter in height.

2 Measure and cut out another rectangle of felt. It should be 0.8 inch (2 cm) shorter and 0.8 inch (2 cm) narrower than the first one. Sew the two rectangles together using a running stitch and brightly colored thread.

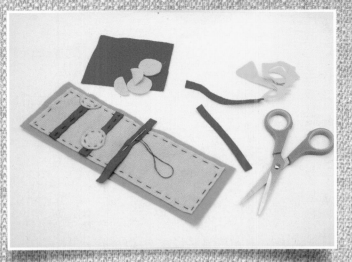

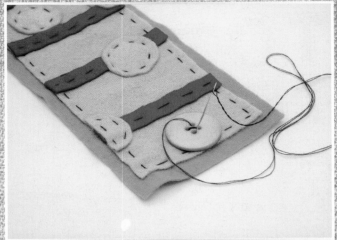

3 Cut some simple shapes out of felt as decorations. Use a tacking stitch to sew them onto the smaller rectangle of felt.

4 Sew a button in the middle of one of the short sides of your rectangle, about 1 inch (3 cm) from the edge.

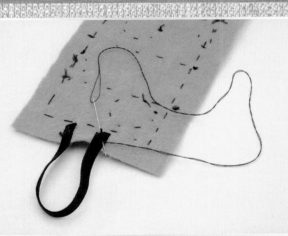

5 Stitch a loop of elastic onto the opposite side of the rectangle from the button. Loop the elastic around the button to fit your cozy onto the mug.

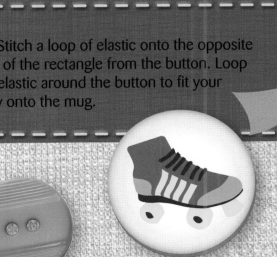

TOTALLY TERRIFIC TOTE

Appliqué is the craft of sewing decorations onto material. It can make something ordinary look unique and original. Decorate a canvas tote using this technique and you will really stand out from the crowd.

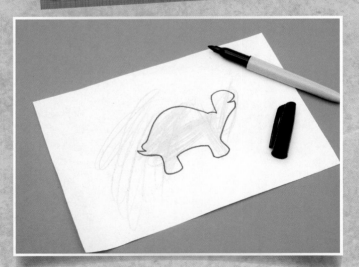

1 Draw a tortoise shape onto a piece of paper using a marker, then cut it out with scissors. This is your template.

2 Pin your paper template onto your fabric, and cut it out. Repeat this four more times using material of different colors.

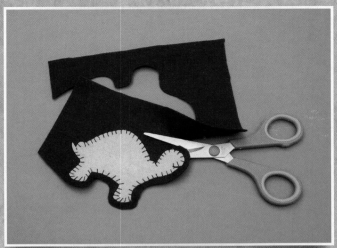

3 Sew four fabric shapes onto the bottom of the bag using a needle and thread. A whip stitch will work nicely. Space them out as evenly as possible.

4 Sew the last fabric shape onto a piece of felt, again using a whip stitch. Cut around it, leaving a 0.4-inch (1 cm) border of felt.

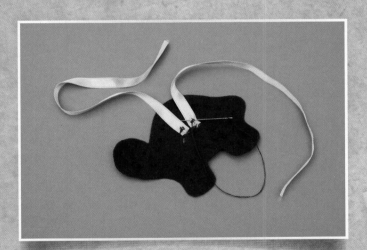

5 Sew two lengths of ribbon to the back of the felt shape. Tie it onto the handle of your canvas bag.

AWESOME ACCESSORIES

Plain gloves and scarves are great for keeping you warm... but they may not look as stylish as you want them to! Why not customize your accessories with ribbon flowers?

You will need:
ribbon
buttons
needle and thread
scarf and gloves
scissors
tape measure

1 Cut a piece of ribbon to a length of 12 inches (30 cm).

2 Sew a loose running stitch along one side of the ribbon, near the edge, leaving the needle still attached.

3 Pull the stitches tight to ruche (frill) the ribbon. Curl the ruched ribbon into a circle and secure it in place with a couple of stitches.

4 Make lots more of these ribbon flowers in different colors.

5 Sew them onto your gloves and scarf by placing a button into the middle of the flower. Stitch in place.

JEAN GENIUS DESK MASCOT

This supersmart mascot will cheer you on when you are studying or taking exams. He won't tell you the answers, though! He is made from an old pair of jeans.

You will need:
- denim from old jeans
- felt
- cushion stuffing
- pins
- needle and thread
- fabric glue
- scissors
- tape measure
- yarn

1 Cut out two 6 x 6-inch (15 x 15 cm) squares of denim, using scissors. Pin them together with the darker side facing inwards.

2 Sew three of the sides together using your needle and thread.

3 Turn the fabric right-side out. Fill it with cushion stuffing. Pinch the middle of the unstitched sides together to make a triangle. Sew along the edge with a running stitch.

4 Cut out different felt decorations for your mascot. You will need eyes, a mouth, a nose, glasses, and a bow tie. Stick these to your mascot with fabric glue.

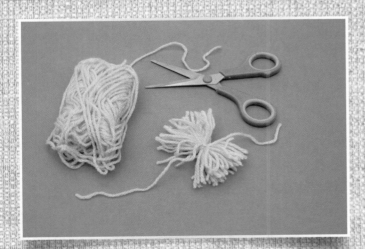

5 Cut a handful of yarn to the same length, and tie it in the middle. Then stitch it onto the top of the mascot, for hair!

SECRET DIARY COVER

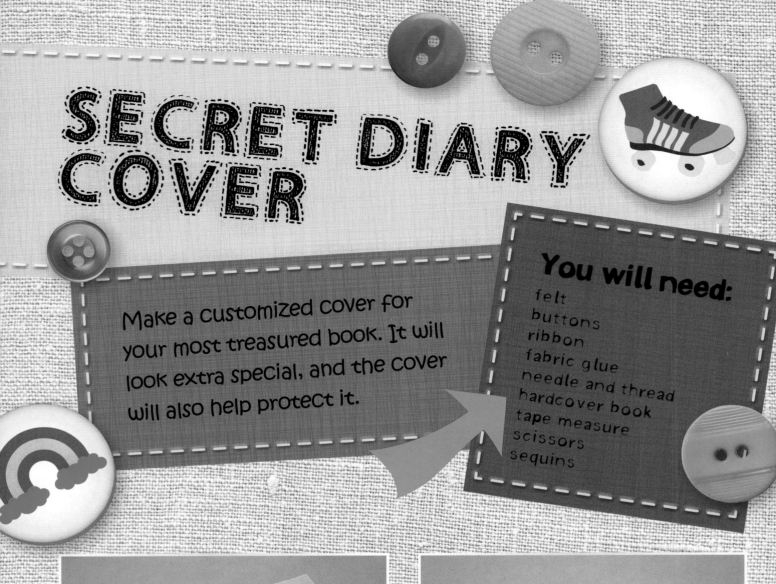

Make a customized cover for your most treasured book. It will look extra special, and the cover will also help protect it.

You will need:
- felt
- buttons
- ribbon
- fabric glue
- needle and thread
- hardcover book
- tape measure
- scissors
- sequins

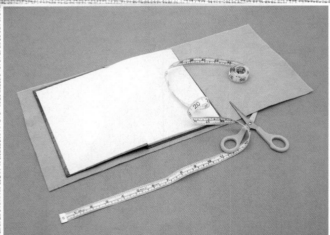

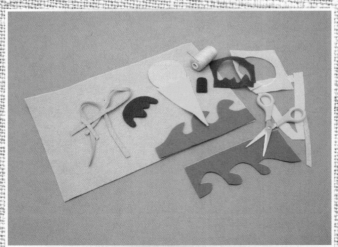

1 Open up your book and measure it. Cut a piece of felt 0.4 inch (1 cm) taller and 2.4 inches (6 cm) wider than the open book.

2 Cut out some felt shapes. You will need some orange strips, a pink circle, a yellow triangle, a blue wave, a brown rectangle, and a red blobby shape (look at the picture!). Sew them in place with a running stitch.

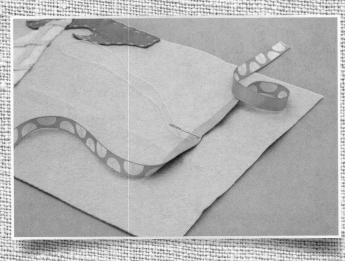

3 Sew on some sequins. Stitch a button about 2.4 inches (6 cm) from the right-hand edge.

4 Cut an 8-inch (20 cm) length of ribbon. Stitch it to the middle of the opposite side of the cover from the button, about 2.4 inches (6 cm) from the edge. Attach it at the middle of the ribbon.

5 Fold over 1 inch (3 cm) of each side. Sew a running stitch at the top and bottom of the folds.

6 Slip the book inside the cover. Tie the ribbon to secure the book.

MINI BAG ORGANIZER

These little storage bags are very handy, and they will look great hanging on your bedroom wall. Now you will always know where your stuff is!

You will need:

cotton fabric
ribbon
cardboard
clothes pins
fabric glue
needle and thread
scissors
tape measure

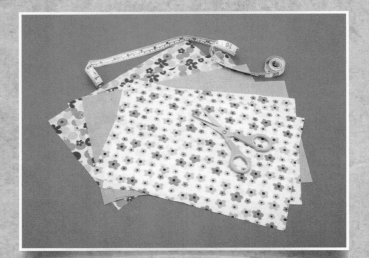

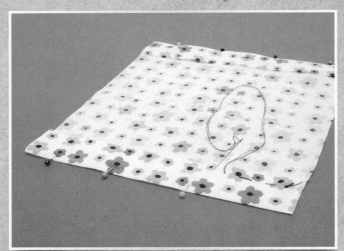

1 Cut six fabric rectangles measuring 8 x 12 inches (20 x 30 cm).

2 Fold the short sides of each rectangle over by 1 inch (3 cm). Sew the folded edges in place with a back stitch.

3 Fold each rectangle in half, with the outside of the cloth facing in. Sew up the two sides with a back stitch. Snip a "V" shape on either side and pass your drawstring ribbon through the holes. Repeat with your other fabric pieces.

4 Cut out a rectangle of cardboard measuring 20 x 16 inches (50 x 40 cm). Then cut out a rectangle of fabric measuring 24 x 20 inches (60 x 50 cm). Fold the edges of the fabric around the card and glue them in place.

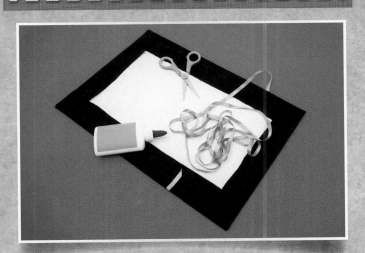

5 Cut two pieces of ribbon 20 inches (50 cm) long. Wrap them around the cardboard and glue the ends down. Hang three clothes pins from each ribbon (see right).

CUPCAKE PINCUSHION

These cute cupcakes look good enough to eat! They are very handy for sticking pins in when you are sewing. But they also look great just as room decorations.

You will need:

silicone cupcake liner
cushion stuffing
felt
shiny beads
fabric glue
needle and thread
scissors
ruler
compass

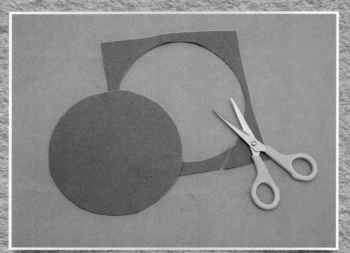

1 Cut out a circle of felt that is 6 inches (15 cm) in diameter. You can measure the circle with a ruler and compass.

2 Cut out a "splotch" shape with wiggly edges that is smaller than the circle. Stitch it on using a running stitch.

3 Sew some shiny beads to the wiggly felt shape with your needle and thread.

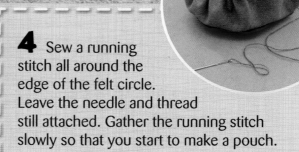

4 Sew a running stitch all around the edge of the felt circle. Leave the needle and thread still attached. Gather the running stitch slowly so that you start to make a pouch.

5 Roll some cushion stuffing in your hands so it makes a ball. Place it in the felt pouch, then pull the running stitch tightly together, and sew the fabric closed. Glue the felt ball into the silicone liner and leave it to dry.

KNITTED PHONE CASE

Knitting is easy to learn. You will get faster with practice, and once you have got the hang of it you can knit all sorts of different things. Start by making a dog case for your phone!

1 Tie your yarn fairly loosely around a knitting needle in a double knot.

2 Pass a second needle through the yarn loop from front to back. This will be the needle in your right hand.

3 Wind the yarn under and over the tip of the right-hand needle and pull firmly. Slide the right-hand needle from behind the left, drawing the yarn through the loop to form a new stitch.

4 Put the new stitch onto the left-hand needle and withdraw the right-hand needle. Pull on the yarn to tighten the stitch. Place the right-hand needle into the back of the stitch you have just made, and then repeat steps 3 and 4 about 30 times.

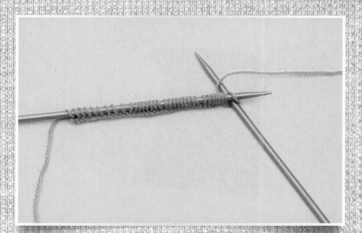

5 With the yarn at the back, slide your right-hand needle into the stitch that is closest to the tip of your left-hand needle, from front to back. Loop the yarn under and over the tip of the right-hand needle.

6 Make a new loop by sliding the tip of the right-hand needle up and over the left. Draw the yarn completely through the stitch on the left-hand needle. Then slip one stitch off of the left-hand needle.

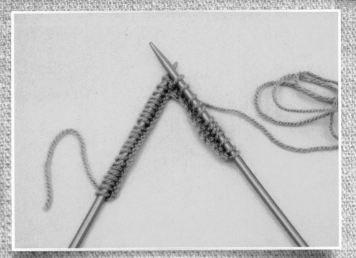

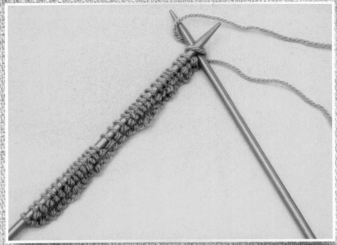

7 Repeat steps 5 and 6. Keep going until you have transferred all the stitches.

8 Swap your needles around and start again. Repeat 20 times until you have made 22 rows in total.

9 Knit two stitches onto the right-hand needle. Use the tip of the first needle to take the first stitch over the second and off the needle. This is called casting off.

10 Make another stitch onto the second needle and repeat. Cast off until you have reached the end of the row and you have one stitch left. Take this off the needle and pull the yarn through the last loop.

11 Fold the rectangle in half and sew up one long and one short side using a darning needle and yarn. Then turn it inside out, to hide your stitches.

12 Cut out felt shapes for your dog's face, and glue them onto your case with fabric glue. Add some googly eyes.

GLOSSARY

compass An instrument for drawing circles, consisting of two arms, one ending in a sharp point and one ending in a pen or pencil.

corduroy A thick cotton fabric with soft parallel raised lines on one side.

mascot An object that it is hoped will bring good luck.

ruched A gather created by passing a running stitch through a length of fabric and pulling the thread tight.

silicone A heat resistant, synthetic material.

tote A large bag.

FURTHER READING

Creative Crafts for Kids: Over 100 Fun Projects for Two to Ten Year Olds by Gill Dickinson, Cheryl Owen, Amanda Grant and Sara Lewis (Hamlyn, 2009)

The Girls' Book of Crafts and Activities (Dorling Kindersley, 2013)

1000 Things to Make and Do (Usborne Publishing Ltd, 2011)

WEBSITES

http://www.education.com/activity/fabric-projects/
Fabric craft projects for kids

http://www.thecraftycrow.net/textiles/
A children's craft collective specializing in crafts found on blogs of people who have worked with kids

http://kidsactivitiesblog.com/9957/textiles-craft-fabric-art
Crafting with scraps of fabric, yard, ribbon and beads

INDEX